mark

D1435903

the gospel according to

mark

authorized king james version

grove press
new york

with an introduction by | barry hannah

1152

*The Pocket Canons were originally published in the U.K. in 1998 by
Canongate Books, Ltd.*
Published simultaneously in Canada
Printed in the United States of America

FIRST AMERICAN EDITION

Copyright information is on file with the Library of Congress
ISBN 0-8021-3617-6

Design by Paddy Cramsie

Grove Press
841 Broadway
New York, NY 10003

99 00 01 02   10 9 8 7 6 5 4 3 2 1

a note about pocket canons

The Authorized King James Version of the Bible, translated between 1603 and 1611, coincided with an extraordinary flowering of English literature. This version, more than any other, and possibly more than any other work in history, has had an influence in shaping the language we speak and write today. Presenting individual books from the Bible as separate volumes, as they were originally conceived, encourages the reader to approach them as literary works in their own right.

The first twelve books in this series encompass categories as diverse as history, fiction, philosophy, love poetry, and law. Each Pocket Canon also has its own introduction, specially commissioned from an impressive range of writers, which provides a personal interpretation of the text and explores its contemporary relevance.

introduction by barry hannah

Mark, leanest of the Gospels, composed around 70 A.D., when the Jewish War saw the destruction of the temple by the army of Titus, was written in a climate of misery and apocalypse. Mark invented the form of the gospel, which means "good news." Yet much of his work countenances despair, doubt, treachery, and death.

These are the same conditions that attend the Turkish earthquake as I write now in the final months of the millennium. Whole cities have collapsed, forty-five thousand body bags have been requested by the government, the rebuilding cost surpasses the state resources, and signs of hope seem far away, even alien.

Mark may have addressed persecuted and refugee Christians of a community in the Roman province of Syria. They looked for an imminent Parousia (second coming) upon the destruction of the temple, and were disappointed when the end had not come, as the scholar Wilfrid Harrington explains.*

This gospel is neglected, and the least quoted. Thomas Jefferson hardly includes material from Mark at all in the Jefferson Bible, wherein he intended to concretize, from the Gospels, "the most sublime and benevolent code of morals which has ever been offered to man." Mark may have seemed

---

* In *Mark*, Collegeville, Minn.: Liturgical Press, 1991.

obscure or elliptical to him. Harrington accounts for the neglect of Mark: "The gospel is uncompromisingly uncomfortable . . . suffering Messiahship and suffering discipleship . . . between the times of resurrection and consummation."

Scholars seem to agree that the most reliable manuscripts of Mark's gospel end at 16:8, not at 16:20, as supplied by many versions. It is helpful to look at the final verses for a tone of the whole gospel:

> And when the sabbath was past, Mary Magdalene, and Mary the mother of James, and Salome, had brought sweet spices, that they might come and anoint him. And very early in the morning the first day of the week, they came into the sepulchre at the rising of the sun. And they said among themselves, "Who shall roll us away the stone at the door of the sepulchre?" And when they looked, they saw the stone was rolled away; for it was very great. And entering the sepulchre, they saw a young man sitting on the right side, clothed in a long white garment; and they were affrighted. And he saith unto them, "Be not affrighted; ye seek Jesus of Nazareth, which was crucified. He is risen; he is not here; behold the place where they laid him. But go your way, tell his disciples and Peter that he goeth before you into Galilee: there shall ye see him, as he said unto you." And they went out quickly, and fled from the sepulchre; for they trembled and were amazed; neither said they any thing to any man; for they were afraid.

There is plainly more fear than hope here, even from the women who have remained faithful throughout the crucifixion while the disciples fled for reasons of personal safety—the very men who dropped their nets to follow Jesus, who saw the healing and the miracles and the walk on water; four of whom heard God speak to Christ from a bright cloud, and one of whom, Peter, the famous denier of Christ three times before the cock crew twice, would be the rock on which Christianity was built. These men could not honor the last hours of Christ by staying awake while he pled with his Father to commute his sentence of death on the cross.

Fear and fatigue, the atheism of evident biology, wherein no man returns from death—these beset the *best* men Christ was able to assemble and appoint as apostles, that is, missionaries of the good news. Judas Iscariot, the crassest and most cowardly of all, has already betrayed Christ to the officials for thirty pieces of silver and then hanged himself in a late attack of conscience. We should remember, however, that Judas *was* a disciple. He was no stranger.

Mark is a book of utter realism, very uncomfortable. It is the vase, basic, without the amplified blooms given to it by the later gospellers Matthew, Luke, and John. The vase, in its abiding economy, has great beauty and holds promise of eternal life, but its theme is heavy on bafflement, misunderstanding, and grief. Even Jesus seems to misunderstand the capabilities of his chosen twelve. He constantly upbraids them and is surprised by their obtuseness. Simply, he has found the men too human—skeptical, cowardly, unimaginative, power seeking, weak. They have quit their professions to follow him, but they never intended to follow him into the precincts of death.

They behave like the deists who had much to do with founding America. God has created the world but then forgotten it. They behave like present bad Christians, like many of us, in fact. The disciples may even be worse than modern believers. They have had hard evidence to believe—visual, aural, physical. We have manuscripts two thousand years old and the testimonies, quite often, of those we dislike and distrust, many who seem a plague of new Pharisees, the screaming Law.

Here is a curious example of the complaint of a modern man against apostles of Christ: Englishman H. E. Arnhold, leading businessman and former chairman of the Shanghai Municipal Council, protests the behavior of a large number of up-country American missionaries in a Japanese internment camp at Chapei (China) during World War II. The missionaries would not comply with camp rules, neglected cleanliness in the lavatories, occupied more floor space than they were entitled to, interfered with the distribution of eggs, and, most annoying of all, propagated the species.

Considering the overcrowded and undernourished condition of the camp one would have thought that self-restraint would have been exercised, so that the camp would not have been deprived of most necessary food (eggs and milk) to provide for this increase in population, apart from the indecency of sexual intercourse in over-crowded dormitories and the embarrassment, annoyance, and disturbance caused to other inmates. . . . One person went through the nightly performance of quoting the Bible to an unwilling spouse until she submitted to his importunities.*

I have never heard Christians accused of being too sexy in public.

Such reportings of the worldly have trailed Christians ever since I have been alive, and there is hardly need to list the more lethal depredations of the Crusades, the Inquisition, the Conquistadors, the Witch Trials, and the collusion of the Vatican with anticommunist fascists, even Hitler; or the late squalor and greed of Jim and Tammy Bakker and Jimmy Swaggart, or other hypocrites and wolves unto the sheep, in order to fill the cyclorama of misdeeds that we are invited to by secular humanists, liberal atheists, and common gleeful wags. We breathe the very air of disbelief and doubt and are currently led by an ostentatious Baptist Bible-toter who delighted in fellatio in the Oval Office just minutes after the funeral of his supposed pal Ron Brown. We did not need to know this, but apparently we adored it when we did. Because we are assured that nobody is better than we are, and this gives comfort to our nasty republican hearts.

But remember that the disciples, constantly upbraided, cowardly, treacherous, obtuse, much weaker than their women, became the apostles of light and went on to their own heroic sufferings, persecutions, jails, and crucifixions.

They were good enough.

* Bernard Wasserstein, *Secret War in Shanghai*, Boston: Houghton Mifflin, 1998, pp. 139-140.

barry hannah

Christ appeared living to them in Galilee and sent them out. They were not only forgiven but adored. They were promised constant friendship and direction by the Savior. This at a time when by all outer appearances the day was doomed, men were confused and abandoned, women huddled in slavish existences, their Savior mocked and destroyed in the humiliating scandal of the cross.

The message of Mark is heartening to bad Christians such as myself, who doubt daily, in our comfort, and even doubt the earthly thing that has brought them the most joy—the writing of stories, in my case. But what serious writer has not doubted the efficacy of words themselves, or their relative courage and truth? We might all be set aside under the leisure section, in the club of idlers and dabblers, of the Great Newspaper in the Sky. Sunday newspaper hell. Such doubts have led to total renunciation of earlier works by born-again converts like Tolstoy, or just rational despair, as with Beckett, who, when bragged upon by some last visitor to his deathbed, said, "But it's just words. Only words. Nothing."

Every day, honest men and women awake to misery, restlessness, doubt, even torture, *if* they awake, and we forget that things were always so, and much worse. We are not in Turkey, dead, or bereft of loved ones overnight. We are in the great nation founded on Christian inclusiveness and forgiveness and tolerance, are we not? That it is an inconceivably wasteful ant colony of Darwinian fascism, the crassest, most materialistic monster the world has ever witnessed, does not occur to us that often, as it does to foreigners, many of whom clamor to enter and drain their brains therein. An exponential amplitude of old Rome, inflicting itself internationally almost with the perfection of flood water.

But it is hopeful to know that not only forgiveness but the power of the Savior's friendship remain available to each unworthy one. And that through the layers of comfort we can reach a decision that will make us happier and the world much better, although Christ has warned that this is the most unlikely decision of all, more difficult than the decision of the early disciples. They were merely fishermen and had only to drop their nets.

Now I offer a poem inspired by Mark's gospel, a brutal and exquisite work, in paravoice of the Savior as I have perceived it.

Do not think so much.
Surrender. Believe.
Unprepared, move out to the world and testify.
The words will come. Serve.
From now on service is kingly.
There are no more kings.
Serve. Help. Love. Others as thyself.
This is impossible but do it.
You have seen enough. You have seen it all,
The miracles, the walk on water, Father speaking
    from a bright cloud.
You were not there but the centurion was,
Through the last hour.
The women, faithful, down the hill, waiting and
    watching.
"Truly this was the Son of God," told the centurion.

barry hannah

To all near the cross. Not you, craven.
The temple did not fall but its veil was rent
Top to bottom. Enough. You do not need the whole
    catastrophe,
For it has already taken place.
God is not in the temple anymore.
You cowards, keep running, but now you are mine,
My brothers and sisters.
Tell them. Help. Love. Service.
My good cowards, weaklings, doubters,
How I love you,
Whom I serve, and will see in Galilee.

I am not aroused to poetry very often but Mark has done
it, with his mysterious compact power. I hope the poem will
be forgiven its deficiencies, as I do not those of my students,
in the spirit of Mark and a recent movie by Robert Duvall,
The Apostle. The movie is exceptional in modern circum-
stances because of its favorable testimony to a Christian
apostle (a murderer) and the power of his tiny church.

The apostle invited everyone to bring their instruments
to the first service. An old black man has brought a trumpet
and blurts on it horribly in praise of the Lord. The apostle
chuckles—one of Duvall's best faces ever—and exclaims
something like "Beautiful!" It put me in mind of Christ himself, in His love for our spirits despite all outward proof.

the gospel according to st mark

The beginning of the gospel of Jesus Christ, the Son of God; ²as it is written in the prophets, 'Behold, I send my messenger before thy face, which shall prepare thy way before thee. ³The voice of one crying in the wilderness, "Prepare ye the way of the Lord, make his paths straight."' ⁴John did baptize in the wilderness, and preach the baptism of repentance for the remission of sins. ⁵And there went out unto him all the land of Judæa, and they of Jerusalem, and were all baptized of him in the river of Jordan, confessing their sins.

⁶And John was clothed with camel's hair, and with a girdle of a skin about his loins; and he did eat locusts and wild honey; ⁷and preached, saying, 'There cometh one mightier than I after me, the latchet of whose shoes I am not worthy to stoop down and unloose. ⁸I indeed have baptized you with water; but he shall baptize you with the Holy Ghost.'

⁹And it came to pass in those days, that Jesus came from Nazareth of Galilee, and was baptized of John in Jordan. ¹⁰And straightway coming up out of the water, he saw the heavens opened, and the Spirit like a dove descending upon him. ¹¹And there came a voice from heaven, saying, 'Thou art my beloved Son, in whom I am well pleased.'

¹²And immediately the Spirit driveth him into the wilderness. ¹³And he was there in the wilderness forty days, tempted

of Satan; and was with the wild beasts; and the angels ministered unto him.

¹⁴ Now after that John was put in prison, Jesus came into Galilee, preaching the gospel of the kingdom of God, ¹⁵ and saying, 'The time is fulfilled, and the kingdom of God is at hand; repent ye, and believe the gospel.'

¹⁶ Now as he walked by the sea of Galilee, he saw Simon and Andrew his brother casting a net into the sea, for they were fishers. ¹⁷And Jesus said unto them, 'Come ye after me, and I will make you to become fishers of men.' ¹⁸And straightway they forsook their nets, and followed him.

¹⁹And when he had gone a little further thence, he saw James the son of Zebedee, and John his brother, who also were in the ship mending their nets. ²⁰And straightway he called them: and they left their father Zebedee in the ship with the hired servants, and went after him.

²¹And they went into Capernaum; and straightway on the sabbath day he entered into the synagogue, and taught. ²²And they were astonished at his doctrine: for he taught them as one that had authority, and not as the scribes. ²³And there was in their synagogue a man with an unclean spirit; and he cried out, ²⁴ saying, 'Let us alone; what have we to do with thee, thou Jesus of Nazareth? Art thou come to destroy us? I know thee who thou art, the Holy One of God.' ²⁵And Jesus rebuked him, saying, 'Hold thy peace, and come out of him.' ²⁶And when the unclean spirit had torn him, and cried with a loud voice, he came out of him. ²⁷And they were all amazed, insomuch that they questioned among themselves, saying, 'What thing is this? What new doctrine is this? For

with authority commandeth he even the unclean spirits, and they do obey him.' ²⁸And immediately his fame spread abroad throughout all the region round about Galilee.

²⁹And forthwith, when they were come out of the synagogue, they entered into the house of Simon and Andrew, with James and John. ³⁰But Simon's wife's mother lay sick of a fever, and anon they tell him of her. ³¹And he came and took her by the hand, and lifted her up; and immediately the fever left her, and she ministered unto them.

³²And at even, when the sun did set, they brought unto him all that were diseased, and them that were possessed with devils. ³³And all the city was gathered together at the door. ³⁴And he healed many that were sick of divers diseases, and cast out many devils; and suffered not the devils to speak, because they knew him.

³⁵And in the morning, rising up a great while before day, he went out, and departed into a solitary place, and there prayed. ³⁶And Simon and they that were with him followed after him. ³⁷And when they had found him, they said unto him, 'All men seek for thee.' ³⁸And he said unto them, 'Let us go into the next towns, that I may preach there also; for therefore came I forth.' ³⁹And he preached in their synagogues throughout all Galilee, and cast out devils.

⁴⁰And there came a leper to him, beseeching him, and kneeling down to him, and saying unto him, 'If thou wilt, thou canst make me clean.' ⁴¹And Jesus, moved with compassion, put forth his hand, and touched him, and saith unto him, 'I will; be thou clean.' ⁴²And as soon as he had spoken, immediately the leprosy departed from him, and he was cleansed.

⁴³And he straitly charged him, and forthwith sent him away; ⁴⁴and saith unto him, 'See thou say nothing to any man; but go thy way, shew thyself to the priest, and offer for thy cleansing those things which Moses commanded, for a testimony unto them.' ⁴⁵But he went out, and began to publish it much, and to blaze abroad the matter, insomuch that Jesus could no more openly enter into the city, but was without in desert places; and they came to him from every quarter.

2 And again he entered into Capernaum after some days; and it was noised that he was in the house. ²And straightway many were gathered together, insomuch that there was no room to receive them, no, not so much as about the door; and he preached the word unto them. ³And they come unto him, bringing one sick of the palsy, which was borne of four. ⁴And when they could not come nigh unto him for the press, they uncovered the roof where he was; and when they had broken it up, they let down the bed wherein the sick of the palsy lay. ⁵When Jesus saw their faith, he said unto the sick of the palsy, 'Son, thy sins be forgiven thee.'

⁶But there were certain of the scribes sitting there, and reasoning in their hearts, ⁷'Why doth this man thus speak blasphemies? Who can forgive sins but God only?' ⁸And immediately when Jesus perceived in his spirit that they so reasoned within themselves, he said unto them, 'Why reason ye these things in your hearts? ⁹Whether is it easier to say to the sick of the palsy, "Thy sins be forgiven thee," or to say, "Arise, and take up thy bed, and walk"? ¹⁰But that ye may know that the Son of man hath power on earth to forgive

sins,' he saith to the sick of the palsy, ¹¹'I say unto thee, Arise, and take up thy bed, and go thy way into thine house.' ¹²And immediately he arose, took up the bed, and went forth before them all; insomuch that they were all amazed, and glorified God, saying, 'We never saw it on this fashion.'

¹³And he went forth again by the sea side; and all the multitude resorted unto him, and he taught them. ¹⁴And as he passed by, he saw Levi the son of Alphæus sitting at the receipt of custom, and said unto him, 'Follow me.' And Levi arose and followed him.

¹⁵And it came to pass, that, as Jesus sat at meat in his house, many publicans and sinners sat also together with Jesus and his disciples; for there were many, and they followed him. ¹⁶And when the scribes and Pharisees saw him eat with publicans and sinners, they said unto his disciples, 'How is it that he eateth and drinketh with publicans and sinners?' ¹⁷When Jesus heard it, he saith unto them, 'They that are whole have no need of the physician, but they that are sick; I came not to call the righteous, but sinners to repentance.'

¹⁸And the disciples of John and of the Pharisees used to fast; and they come and say unto him, 'Why do the disciples of John and of the Pharisees fast, but thy disciples fast not?' ¹⁹And Jesus said unto them, 'Can the children of the bridechamber fast, while the bridegroom is with them? As long as they have the bridegroom with them, they cannot fast. ²⁰But the days will come, when the bridegroom shall be taken away from them, and then shall they fast in those days.

²¹'No man also seweth a piece of new cloth on an old garment; else the new piece that filled it up taketh away from

the old, and the rent is made worse. ²²And no man putteth new wine into old bottles; else the new wine doth burst the bottles, and the wine is spilled, and the bottles will be marred; but new wine must be put into new bottles.' ²³And it came to pass that he went through the corn fields on the sabbath day; and his disciples began, as they went, to pluck the ears of corn. ²⁴And the Pharisees said unto him, 'Behold, why do they on the sabbath day that which is not lawful?' ²⁵And he said unto them, 'Have ye never read what David did, when he had need, and was an hungred, he, and they that were with him? ²⁶How he went into the house of God in the days of Abiathar the high priest, and did eat the shewbread, which is not lawful to eat but for the priests, and gave also to them which were with him?'

²⁷And he said unto them, 'The sabbath was made for man, and not man for the sabbath; ²⁸therefore the Son of man is Lord also of the sabbath.'

3 And he entered again into the synagogue; and there was a man there which had a withered hand. ²And they watched him, whether he would heal him on the sabbath day; that they might accuse him.

³And he saith unto the man which had the withered hand, 'Stand forth.' ⁴And he saith unto them, 'Is it lawful to do good on the sabbath days, or to do evil? To save life, or to kill?' But they held their peace. ⁵And when he had looked round about on them with anger, being grieved for the hardness of their hearts, he saith unto the man, 'Stretch forth thine hand.' And he stretched it out; and his hand was restored

whole as the other. ⁶And the Pharisees went forth, and straightway took counsel with the Herodians against him, how they might destroy him.

⁷But Jesus withdrew himself with his disciples to the sea; and a great multitude from Galilee followed him, and from Judæa, ⁸and from Jerusalem, and from Idumæa, and from beyond Jordan; and they about Tyre and Sidon, a great multitude, when they had heard what great things he did, came unto him. ⁹And he spake to his disciples, that a small ship should wait on him because of the multitude, lest they should throng him. ¹⁰For he had healed many; insomuch that they pressed upon him for to touch him, as many as had plagues. ¹¹And unclean spirits, when they saw him, fell down before him, and cried, saying, 'Thou art the Son of God.' ¹²And he straitly charged them that they should not make him known.

¹³And he goeth up into a mountain, and calleth unto him whom he would: and they came unto him. ¹⁴And he ordained twelve, that they should be with him, and that he might send them forth to preach, ¹⁵and to have power to heal sicknesses, and to cast out devils: ¹⁶and Simon he surnamed Peter; ¹⁷and James the son of Zebedee, and John the brother of James; and he surnamed them Boanerges, which is, The sons of thunder; ¹⁸and Andrew, and Philip, and Bartholomew, and Matthew, and Thomas, and James the son of Alphæus, and Thaddæus, and Simon the Canaanite; ¹⁹and Judas Iscariot, which also betrayed him. And they went into an house. ²⁰And the multitude cometh together again, so that they could not so much as eat bread. ²¹And when his friends heard of it, they went out to lay hold on him; for they said, 'He is beside himself.'

²²And the scribes which came down from Jerusalem said, 'He hath Beelzebub, and by the prince of the devils casteth he out devils.' ²³And he called them unto him, and said unto them in parables, 'How can Satan cast out Satan? ²⁴And if a kingdom be divided against itself, that kingdom cannot stand. ²⁵And if a house be divided against itself, that house cannot stand. ²⁶And if Satan rise up against himself, and be divided, he cannot stand, but hath an end.

²⁷'No man can enter into a strong man's house, and spoil his goods, except he will first bind the strong man; and then he will spoil his house.

²⁸'Verily I say unto you, all sins shall be forgiven unto the sons of men, and blasphemies wherewith soever they shall blaspheme; ²⁹but he that shall blaspheme against the Holy Ghost hath never forgiveness, but is in danger of eternal damnation, ³⁰because they said, "He hath an unclean spirit."'

³¹There came then his brethren and his mother, and, standing without, sent unto him, calling him. ³²And the multitude sat about him, and they said unto him, 'Behold, thy mother and thy brethren without seek for thee.' ³³And he answered them, saying, 'Who is my mother, or my brethren?' ³⁴And he looked round about on them which sat about him, and said, 'Behold my mother and my brethren! ³⁵For whosoever shall do the will of God, the same is my brother, and my sister, and mother.'

4 And he began again to teach by the sea side; and there was gathered unto him a great multitude, so that he entered into a ship, and sat in the sea; and the whole multitude

was by the sea on the land. ²And he taught them many things by parables, and said unto them in his doctrine, ³ 'Hearken; behold, there went out a sower to sow. ⁴And it came to pass, as he sowed, some fell by the way side, and the fowls of the air came and devoured it up. ⁵And some fell on stony ground, where it had not much earth; and immediately it sprang up, because it had no depth of earth. ⁶But when the sun was up, it was scorched; and because it had no root, it withered away. ⁷And some fell among thorns, and the thorns grew up, and choked it, and it yielded no fruit. ⁸And other fell on good ground, and did yield fruit that sprang up and increased; and brought forth, some thirty, and some sixty, and some an hundred.' ⁹And he said unto them, 'He that hath ears to hear, let him hear.'

¹⁰And when he was alone, they that were about him with the twelve asked of him the parable. ¹¹And he said unto them, 'Unto you it is given to know the mystery of the kingdom of God; but unto them that are without, all these things are done in parables; ¹²that seeing they may see, and not perceive; and hearing they may hear, and not understand; lest at any time they should be converted, and their sins should be forgiven them.'

¹³And he said unto them, 'Know ye not this parable? And how then will ye know all parables?

¹⁴ 'The sower soweth the word. ¹⁵And these are they by the way side, where the word is sown; but when they have heard, Satan cometh immediately, and taketh away the word that was sown in their hearts. ¹⁶And these are they likewise which are sown on stony ground; who, when they have

heard the word, immediately receive it with gladness; [17]and have no root in themselves, and so endure but for a time; afterward, when affliction or persecution ariseth for the word's sake, immediately they are offended. [18]And these are they which are sown among thorns; such as hear the word, [19]and the cares of this world, and the deceitfulness of riches, and the lusts of other things entering in, choke the word, and it becometh unfruitful. [20]And these are they which are sown on good ground; such as hear the word, and receive it, and bring forth fruit, some thirtyfold, some sixty, and some an hundred.'

[21]And he said unto them, 'Is a candle brought to be put under a bushel, or under a bed? And not to be set on a candlestick? [22]For there is nothing hid, which shall not be manifested; neither was any thing kept secret, but that it should come abroad. [23]If any man have ears to hear, let him hear.' [24]And he said unto them, 'Take heed what ye hear: with what measure ye mete, it shall be measured to you; and unto you that hear shall more be given. [25]For he that hath, to him shall be given; and he that hath not, from him shall be taken even that which he hath.'

[26]And he said, 'So is the kingdom of God, as if a man should cast seed into the ground; [27]and should sleep, and rise night and day, and the seed should spring and grow up, he knoweth not how. [28]For the earth bringeth forth fruit of herself; first the blade, then the ear, after that the full corn in the ear. [29]But when the fruit is brought forth, immediately he putteth in the sickle, because the harvest is come.'

[30]And he said, 'Whereunto shall we liken the kingdom of

God? Or with what comparison shall we compare it? [31] It is like a grain of mustard seed, which, when it is sown in the earth, is less than all the seeds that be in the earth; [32] but when it is sown, it groweth up, and becometh greater than all herbs, and shooteth out great branches; so that the fowls of the air may lodge under the shadow of it.'

[33] And with many such parables spake he the word unto them, as they were able to hear it. [34] But without a parable spake he not unto them; and when they were alone, he expounded all things to his disciples.

[35] And the same day, when the even was come, he saith unto them, 'Let us pass over unto the other side.' [36] And when they had sent away the multitude, they took him even as he was in the ship. And there were also with him other little ships. [37] And there arose a great storm of wind, and the waves beat into the ship, so that it was now full. [38] And he was in the hinder part of the ship, asleep on a pillow; and they awake him, and say unto him, 'Master, carest thou not that we perish?' [39] And he arose, and rebuked the wind, and said unto the sea, 'Peace, be still.' And the wind ceased, and there was a great calm. [40] And he said unto them, 'Why are ye so fearful? How is it that ye have no faith?' [41] And they feared exceedingly, and said one to another, 'What manner of man is this, that even the wind and the sea obey him?'

5 And they came over unto the other side of the sea, into the country of the Gadarenes. [2] And when he was come out of the ship, immediately there met him out of the tombs a man with an unclean spirit, [3] who had his dwelling among

the tombs; and no man could bind him, no, not with chains; [4]because that he had been often bound with fetters and chains, and the chains had been plucked asunder by him, and the fetters broken in pieces; neither could any man tame him.

[5]And always, night and day, he was in the mountains, and in the tombs, crying, and cutting himself with stones. [6]But when he saw Jesus afar off, he ran and worshipped him, [7]and cried with a loud voice, and said, 'What have I to do with thee, Jesus, thou Son of the most high God? I adjure thee by God, that thou torment me not.' [8]For Jesus said unto him, 'Come out of the man, thou unclean spirit.' [9]And he asked him, 'What is thy name?' And the man answered, saying, 'My name is Legion: for we are many.' [10]And he besought him much that he would not send them away out of the country.

[11]Now there was there nigh unto the mountains a great herd of swine feeding. [12]And all the devils besought him, saying, 'Send us into the swine, that we may enter into them.' [13]And forthwith Jesus gave them leave. And the unclean spirits went out, and entered into the swine; and the herd ran violently down a steep place into the sea (they were about two thousand) and were choked in the sea.

[14]And they that fed the swine fled, and told it in the city, and in the country. And they went out to see what it was that was done. [15]And they come to Jesus, and see him that was possessed with the devil, and had the legion, sitting, and clothed, and in his right mind; and they were afraid. [16]And they that saw it told them how it befell to him that was possessed with the devil, and also concerning the swine. [17]And

they began to pray him to depart out of their coasts. [18]And when he was come into the ship, he that had been possessed with the devil prayed him that he might be with him. [19]Howbeit Jesus suffered him not, but saith unto him, 'Go home to thy friends, and tell them how great things the Lord hath done for thee, and hath had compassion on thee.' [20]And he departed, and began to publish in Decapolis how great things Jesus had done for him; and all men did marvel.

[21]And when Jesus was passed over again by ship unto the other side, much people gathered unto him: and he was nigh unto the sea. [22]And, behold, there cometh one of the rulers of the synagogue, Jairus by name; and when he saw him, he fell at his feet, [23]and besought him greatly, saying, 'My little daughter lieth at the point of death; I pray thee, come and lay thy hands on her, that she may be healed; and she shall live.' [24]And Jesus went with him; and much people followed him, and thronged him.

[25]And a certain woman, which had an issue of blood twelve years, [26]and had suffered many things of many physicians, and had spent all that she had, and was nothing bettered, but rather grew worse, [27]when she had heard of Jesus, came in the press behind, and touched his garment. [28]For she said, 'If I may touch but his clothes, I shall be whole.' [29]And straightway the fountain of her blood was dried up; and she felt in her body that she was healed of that plague. [30]And Jesus, immediately knowing in himself that virtue had gone out of him, turned him about in the press, and said, 'Who touched my clothes?' [31]And his disciples said unto him, 'Thou seest the multitude thronging thee, and sayest thou, "Who touched me?"'

³²And he looked round about to see her that had done this thing. ³³But the woman fearing and trembling, knowing what was done in her, came and fell down before him, and told him all the truth. ³⁴And he said unto her, 'Daughter, thy faith hath made thee whole; go in peace, and be whole of thy plague.'

³⁵While he yet spake, there came from the ruler of the synagogue's house certain which said, 'Thy daughter is dead; why troublest thou the Master any further?' ³⁶As soon as Jesus heard the word that was spoken, he saith unto the ruler of the synagogue, 'Be not afraid, only believe.' ³⁷And he suffered no man to follow him, save Peter, and James, and John the brother of James. ³⁸And he cometh to the house of the ruler of the synagogue, and seeth the tumult, and them that wept and wailed greatly. ³⁹And when he was come in, he saith unto them, 'Why make ye this ado, and weep? The damsel is not dead, but sleepeth.' ⁴⁰And they laughed him to scorn. But when he had put them all out, he taketh the father and the mother of the damsel, and them that were with him, and entereth in where the damsel was lying. ⁴¹And he took the damsel by the hand, and said unto her, 'Talitha cumi,' which is, being interpreted, 'Damsel, I say unto thee, arise.' ⁴²And straightway the damsel arose, and walked; for she was of the age of twelve years. And they were astonished with a great astonishment. ⁴³And he charged them straitly that no man should know it; and commanded that something should be given her to eat.

6 And he went out from thence, and came into his own country; and his disciples follow him. ²And when the

sabbath day was come, he began to teach in the synagogue; and many hearing him were astonished, saying, 'From whence hath this man these things? And what wisdom is this which is given unto him, that even such mighty works are wrought by his hands? ³Is not this the carpenter, the son of Mary, the brother of James, and Joses, and of Juda, and Simon? And are not his sisters here with us?' And they were offended at him. ⁴But Jesus said unto them, 'A prophet is not without honour, but in his own country, and among his own kin, and in his own house.' ⁵And he could there do no mighty work, save that he laid his hands upon a few sick folk, and healed them. ⁶And he marvelled because of their unbelief. And he went round about the villages, teaching.

⁷And he called unto him the twelve, and began to send them forth by two and two; and gave them power over unclean spirits; ⁸and commanded them that they should take nothing for their journey, save a staff only; no scrip, no bread, no money in their purse; ⁹but be shod with sandals; and not put on two coats. ¹⁰And he said unto them, 'In what place soever ye enter into an house, there abide till ye depart from that place. ¹¹And whosoever shall not receive you, nor hear you, when ye depart thence, shake off the dust under your feet for a testimony against them. Verily I say unto you, It shall be more tolerable for Sodom and Gomorrha in the day of judgment, than for that city.' ¹²And they went out, and preached that men should repent. ¹³And they cast out many devils, and anointed with oil many that were sick, and healed them.

¹⁴And king Herod heard of him (for his name was spread abroad) and he said, 'That John the Baptist was risen from

the dead, and therefore mighty works do shew forth them-selves in him.' ¹⁵ Others said, 'That it is Elias.' And others said, 'That it is a prophet, or as one of the prophets.' ¹⁶ But when Herod heard thereof, he said, 'It is John, whom I beheaded; he is risen from the dead.'

¹⁷ For Herod himself had sent forth and laid hold upon John, and bound him in prison for Herodias' sake, his brother Philip's wife; for he had married her. ¹⁸ For John had said unto Herod, 'It is not lawful for thee to have thy brother's wife.' ¹⁹ Therefore Herodias had a quarrel against him, and would have killed him; but she could not; ²⁰ for Herod feared John, knowing that he was a just man and an holy, and observed him; and when he heard him, he did many things, and heard him gladly.

²¹ And when a convenient day was come, that Herod on his birthday made a supper to his lords, high captains, and chief estates of Galilee; ²² and when the daughter of the said Herodias came in, and danced, and pleased Herod and them that sat with him, the king said unto the damsel, 'Ask of me whatsoever thou wilt, and I will give it thee.' ²³ And he sware unto her, 'Whatsoever thou shalt ask of me, I will give it thee, unto the half of my kingdom.' ²⁴ And she went forth, and said unto her mother, 'What shall I ask?' And she said, 'The head of John the Baptist.' ²⁵ And she came in straight-way with haste unto the king, and asked, saying, 'I will that thou give me by and by in a charger the head of John the Baptist.' ²⁶ And the king was exceeding sorry; yet for his oath's sake, and for their sakes which sat with him, he would not reject her. ²⁷ And immediately the king sent an executioner,

and commanded his head to be brought; and he went and beheaded him in the prison, ²⁸and brought his head in a charger, and gave it to the damsel; and the damsel gave it to her mother.

²⁹And when his disciples heard of it, they came and took up his corpse, and laid it in a tomb.

³⁰And the apostles gathered themselves together unto Jesus, and told him all things, both what they had done, and what they had taught. ³¹And he said unto them, 'Come ye yourselves apart into a desert place, and rest a while,' for there were many coming and going, and they had no leisure so much as to eat. ³²And they departed into a desert place by ship privately. ³³And the people saw them departing, and many knew him, and ran afoot thither out of all cities, and outwent them, and came together unto him. ³⁴And Jesus, when he came out, saw much people, and was moved with compassion toward them, because they were as sheep not having a shepherd; and he began to teach them many things. ³⁵And when the day was now far spent, his disciples came unto him, and said, 'This is a desert place, and now the time is far passed; ³⁶send them away, that they may go into the country round about, and into the villages, and buy themselves bread; for they have nothing to eat.' ³⁷He answered and said unto them, 'Give ye them to eat.' And they say unto him, 'Shall we go and buy two hundred pennyworth of bread, and give them to eat?' ³⁸He saith unto them, 'How many loaves have ye? Go and see.' And when they knew, they say, 'Five, and two fishes.' ³⁹And he commanded them to make all sit down by companies upon the green grass. ⁴⁰And they

sat down in ranks, by hundreds, and by fifties. ⁴¹And when he had taken the five loaves and the two fishes, he looked up to heaven, and blessed, and brake the loaves, and gave them to his disciples to set before them; and the two fishes divided he among them all. ⁴²And they did all eat, and were filled. ⁴³And they took up twelve baskets full of the fragments, and of the fishes. ⁴⁴And they that did eat of the loaves were about five thousand men.

⁴⁵And straightway he constrained his disciples to get into the ship, and to go to the other side before unto Bethsaida, while he sent away the people. ⁴⁶And when he had sent them away, he departed into a mountain to pray. ⁴⁷And when even was come, the ship was in the midst of the sea, and he alone on the land. ⁴⁸And he saw them toiling in rowing; for the wind was contrary unto them; and about the fourth watch of the night he cometh unto them, walking upon the sea, and would have passed by them. ⁴⁹But when they saw him walking upon the sea, they supposed it had been a spirit, and cried out; ⁵⁰for they all saw him, and were troubled. And immediately he talked with them, and saith unto them, 'Be of good cheer: it is I; be not afraid.' ⁵¹And he went up unto them into the ship; and the wind ceased; and they were sore amazed in themselves beyond measure, and wondered. ⁵²For they considered not the miracle of the loaves; for their heart was hardened.

⁵³And when they had passed over, they came into the land of Gennesaret, and drew to the shore. ⁵⁴And when they were come out of the ship, straightway they knew him, ⁵⁵and ran through that whole region round about, and began to

carry about in beds those that were sick, where they heard he was. ⁵⁶And whithersoever he entered, into villages, or cities, or country, they laid the sick in the streets, and besought him that they might touch if it were but the border of his garment: and as many as touched him were made whole.

7 Then came together unto him the Pharisees, and certain of the scribes, which came from Jerusalem. ²And when they saw some of his disciples eat bread with defiled, that is to say, with unwashen, hands, they found fault. ³For the Pharisees, and all the Jews, except they wash their hands oft, eat not, holding the tradition of the elders. ⁴And when they come from the market, except they wash, they eat not. And many other things there be, which they have received to hold, as the washing of cups, and pots, brasen vessels, and of tables. ⁵Then the Pharisees and scribes asked him, 'Why walk not thy disciples according to the tradition of the elders, but eat bread with unwashen hands?' ⁶He answered and said unto them, 'Well hath Esaias prophesied of you hypocrites, as it is written, "This people honoureth me with their lips, but their heart is far from me. ⁷Howbeit in vain do they worship me, teaching for doctrines the commandments of men." ⁸For laying aside the commandment of God, ye hold the tradition of men, as the washing of pots and cups; and many other such like things ye do.'

⁹And he said unto them, 'Full well ye reject the commandment of God, that ye may keep your own tradition. ¹⁰For Moses said, "Honour thy father and thy mother," and, "Whoso curseth father or mother, let him die the death." ¹¹But ye

say, "If a man shall say to his father or mother, 'It is Corban,'
that is to say, a gift, by whatsoever thou mightest be profited
by me; he shall be free." ¹²And ye suffer him no more to do
ought for his father or his mother; ¹³ making the word of God
of none effect through your tradition, which ye have delivered: and many such like things do ye.'

¹⁴And when he had called all the people unto him, he said
unto them, 'Hearken unto me every one of you, and understand: ¹⁵ there is nothing from without a man, that entering
into him can defile him; but the things which come out of
him, those are they that defile the man. ¹⁶ If any man have
ears to hear, let him hear.'

¹⁷And when he was entered into the house from the people, his disciples asked him concerning the parable. ¹⁸And he
saith unto them, 'Are ye so without understanding also? Do
ye not perceive, that whatsoever thing from without entereth into the man, it cannot defile him; ¹⁹ because it entereth
not into his heart, but into the belly, and goeth out into the
draught, purging all meats?' ²⁰And he said, 'That which
cometh out of the man, that defileth the man. ²¹ For from
within, out of the heart of men, proceed evil thoughts, adul-
teries, fornications, murders, ²² thefts, covetousness, wicked-
ness, deceit, lasciviousness, an evil eye, blasphemy, pride,
foolishness: ²³ all these evil things come from within, and
defile the man.'

²⁴And from thence he arose, and went into the borders of
Tyre and Sidon, and entered into an house, and would have
no man know it; but he could not be hid. ²⁵ For a certain
woman, whose young daughter had an unclean spirit, heard

of him, and came and fell at his feet. ^{26} The woman was a Greek, a Syrophenician by nation; and she besought him that he would cast forth the devil out of her daughter. ^{27} But Jesus said unto her, 'Let the children first be filled: for it is not meet to take the children's bread, and to cast it unto the dogs.' ^{28} And she answered and said unto him, 'Yes, Lord: yet the dogs under the table eat of the children's crumbs.' ^{29} And he said unto her, 'For this saying go thy way; the devil is gone out of thy daughter.' ^{30} And when she was come to her house, she found the devil gone out, and her daughter laid upon the bed.

^{31} And again, departing from the coasts of Tyre and Sidon, he came unto the sea of Galilee, through the midst of the coasts of Decapolis. ^{32} And they bring unto him one that was deaf, and had an impediment in his speech; and they beseech him to put his hand upon him. ^{33} And he took him aside from the multitude, and put his fingers into his ears, and he spit, and touched his tongue; ^{34} and looking up to heaven, he sighed, and saith unto him, 'Ephphatha,' that is, 'Be opened.' ^{35} And straightway his ears were opened, and the string of his tongue was loosed, and he spake plain. ^{36} And he charged them that they should tell no man; but the more he charged them, so much the more a great deal they published it; ^{37} and were beyond measure astonished, saying, 'He hath done all things well: he maketh both the deaf to hear, and the dumb to speak.'

8 In those days the multitude being very great, and having nothing to eat, Jesus called his disciples unto him, and saith unto them, ² 'I have compassion on the multitude, because they have now been with me three days, and have nothing to eat; ³ and if I send them away fasting to their own houses, they will faint by the way; for divers of them came from far.' ⁴ And his disciples answered him, 'From whence can a man satisfy these men with bread here in the wilderness?' ⁵ And he asked them, 'How many loaves have ye?' And they said, 'Seven.' ⁶ And he commanded the people to sit down on the ground: and he took the seven loaves, and gave thanks, and brake, and gave to his disciples to set before them; and they did set them before the people. ⁷ And they had a few small fishes; and he blessed, and commanded to set them also before them. ⁸ So they did eat, and were filled; and they took up of the broken meat that was left seven baskets. ⁹ And they that had eaten were about four thousand; and he sent them away.

¹⁰ And straightway he entered into a ship with his disciples, and came into the parts of Dalmanutha. ¹¹ And the Pharisees came forth, and began to question with him, seeking of him a sign from heaven, tempting him. ¹² And he sighed deeply in his spirit, and saith, 'Why doth this generation seek after a sign? Verily I say unto you, There shall no sign be given unto this generation.' ¹³ And he left them, and entering into the ship again departed to the other side.

¹⁴ Now the disciples had forgotten to take bread, neither had they in the ship with them more than one loaf. ¹⁵ And he charged them, saying, 'Take heed, beware of the leaven of the Pharisees, and of the leaven of Herod.' ¹⁶ And they reasoned among themselves, saying, 'It is because we have no

bread.' [17]And when Jesus knew it, he saith unto them, 'Why reason ye, because ye have no bread? Perceive ye not yet, neither understand? Have ye your heart yet hardened? [18]Having eyes, see ye not? And having ears, hear ye not? And do ye not remember? [19]When I brake the five loaves among five thousand, how many baskets full of fragments took ye up?' They say unto him, 'Twelve.' [20]'And when the seven among four thousand, how many baskets full of fragments took ye up?' And they said, 'Seven.' [21]And he said unto them, 'How is it that ye do not understand?'

[22]And he cometh to Bethsaida; and they bring a blind man unto him, and besought him to touch him. [23]And he took the blind man by the hand, and led him out of the town; and when he had spit on his eyes, and put his hands upon him, he asked him if he saw ought. [24]And he looked up, and said, 'I see men as trees, walking.' [25]After that he put his hands again upon his eyes, and made him look up: and he was restored, and saw every man clearly. [26]And Jesus sent him away to his house, saying, 'Neither go into the town, nor tell it to any in the town.'

[27]And Jesus went out, and his disciples, into the towns of Cæsarea Philippi: and by the way he asked his disciples, saying unto them, 'Whom do men say that I am?' [28]And they answered, 'John the Baptist: but some say, Elias; and others, one of the prophets.' [29]And he saith unto them, 'But whom say ye that I am?' And Peter answereth and saith unto him, 'Thou art the Christ.' [30]And he charged them that they should tell no man of him. [31]And he began to teach them, that the Son of man must suffer many things, and be rejected of the

elders, and of the chief priests, and scribes, and be killed, and after three days rise again. ³²And he spake that saying openly. And Peter took him, and began to rebuke him. ³³But when he had turned about and looked on his disciples, he rebuked Peter, saying, 'Get thee behind me, Satan: for thou savourest not the things that be of God, but the things that be of men.'

³⁴And when he had called the people unto him with his disciples also, he said unto them, 'Whosoever will come after me, let him deny himself, and take up his cross, and follow me. ³⁵For whosoever will save his life shall lose it; but whosoever shall lose his life for my sake and the gospel's, the same shall save it. ³⁶For what shall it profit a man, if he shall gain the whole world, and lose his own soul? ³⁷Or what shall a man give in exchange for his soul? ³⁸Whosoever therefore shall be ashamed of me and of my words in this adulterous and sinful generation; of him also shall the Son of man be ashamed, when he cometh in the glory of his Father with the holy angels.'

9 And he said unto them, 'Verily I say unto you, that there be some of them that stand here, which shall not taste of death, till they have seen the kingdom of God come with power.'

²And after six days Jesus taketh with him Peter, and James, and John, and leadeth them up into an high mountain apart by themselves; and he was transfigured before them. ³And his raiment became shining, exceeding white as snow; so as no fuller on earth can white them. ⁴And there appeared unto

them Elias with Moses; and they were talking with Jesus. [5] And Peter answered and said to Jesus, 'Master, it is good for us to be here; and let us make three tabernacles: one for thee, and one for Moses, and one for Elias.' [6] For he wist not what to say; for they were sore afraid. [7] And there was a cloud that overshadowed them; and a voice came out of the cloud, saying, 'This is my beloved Son: hear him.' [8] And suddenly, when they had looked round about, they saw no man any more, save Jesus only with themselves. [9] And as they came down from the mountain, he charged them that they should tell no man what things they had seen, till the Son of man were risen from the dead. [10] And they kept that saying with themselves, questioning one with another what the rising from the dead should mean.

[11] And they asked him, saying, 'Why say the scribes that Elias must first come?' [12] And he answered and told them, 'Elias verily cometh first, and restoreth all things; and how it is written of the Son of man, that he must suffer many things, and be set at nought. [13] But I say unto you, that Elias is indeed come, and they have done unto him whatsoever they listed, as it is written of him.'

[14] And when he came to his disciples, he saw a great multitude about them, and the scribes questioning with them. [15] And straightway all the people, when they beheld him, were greatly amazed, and running to him saluted him. [16] And he asked the scribes, 'What question ye with them?' [17] And one of the multitude answered and said, 'Master, I have brought unto thee my son, which hath a dumb spirit; [18] and wheresoever he taketh him, he teareth him: and he foameth,

and gnasheth with his teeth, and pineth away; and I spake to thy disciples that they should cast him out; and they could not.' ¹⁹He answereth him, and saith, 'O faithless generation, how long shall I be with you? How long shall I suffer you? Bring him unto me.' ²⁰And they brought him unto him: and when he saw him, straightway the spirit tare him; and he fell on the ground, and wallowed foaming. ²¹And he asked his father, 'How long is it ago since this came unto him?' And he said, 'Of a child. ²²And ofttimes it hath cast him into the fire, and into the waters, to destroy him; but if thou canst do any thing, have compassion on us, and help us.' ²³Jesus said unto him, 'If thou canst believe, all things are possible to him that believeth.' ²⁴And straightway the father of the child cried out, and said with tears, 'Lord, I believe; help thou mine unbelief.' ²⁵When Jesus saw that the people came running together, he rebuked the foul spirit, saying unto him, 'Thou dumb and deaf spirit, I charge thee, come out of him, and enter no more into him.' ²⁶And the spirit cried, and rent him sore, and came out of him: and he was as one dead; insomuch that many said, 'He is dead.' ²⁷But Jesus took him by the hand, and lifted him up; and he arose. ²⁸And when he was come into the house, his disciples asked him privately, 'Why could not we cast him out?' ²⁹And he said unto them, 'This kind can come forth by nothing, but by prayer and fasting.'

³⁰And they departed thence, and passed through Galilee; and he would not that any man should know it. ³¹For he taught his disciples, and said unto them, 'The Son of man is delivered into the hands of men, and they shall kill him; and after that he is killed, he shall rise the third day.' ³²But they

understood not that saying, and were afraid to ask him.

³³And he came to Capernaum: and being in the house he asked them, 'What was it that ye disputed among yourselves by the way?' ³⁴But they held their peace: for by the way they had disputed among themselves, who should be the greatest. ³⁵And he sat down, and called the twelve, and saith unto them, 'If any man desire to be first, the same shall be last of all, and servant of all.' ³⁶And he took a child, and set him in the midst of them; and when he had taken him in his arms, he said unto them, ³⁷'Whosoever shall receive one of such children in my name, receiveth me; and whosoever shall receive me, receiveth not me, but him that sent me.'

³⁸And John answered him, saying, 'Master, we saw one casting out devils in thy name, and he followeth not us; and we forbad him, because he followeth not us.' ³⁹But Jesus said, 'Forbid him not; for there is no man which shall do a miracle in my name, that can lightly speak evil of me. ⁴⁰For he that is not against us is on our part. ⁴¹For whosoever shall give you a cup of water to drink in my name, because ye belong to Christ, verily I say unto you, he shall not lose his reward.

⁴²'And whosoever shall offend one of these little ones that believe in me, it is better for him that a millstone were hanged about his neck, and he were cast into the sea. ⁴³And if thy hand offend thee, cut it off; it is better for thee to enter into life maimed, than having two hands to go into hell, into the fire that never shall be quenched, ⁴⁴where their worm dieth not, and the fire is not quenched. ⁴⁵And if thy foot offend thee, cut it off: it is better for thee to enter halt into life, than having two feet to be cast into hell, into the fire that

never shall be quenched, ⁴⁶ where their worm dieth not, and the fire is not quenched. ⁴⁷And if thine eye offend thee, pluck it out; it is better for thee to enter into the kingdom of God with one eye, than having two eyes to be cast into hell fire, ⁴⁸ where their worm dieth not, and the fire is not quenched. ⁴⁹ For every one shall be salted with fire, and every sacrifice shall be salted with salt. ⁵⁰ Salt is good; but if the salt have lost his saltness, wherewith will ye season it? Have salt in yourselves, and have peace one with another.'

10

And he arose from thence, and cometh into the coasts of Judæa by the farther side of Jordan; and the people resort unto him again; and, as he was wont, he taught them again.

²And the Pharisees came to him, and asked him, 'Is it lawful for a man to put away his wife?' tempting him. ³And he answered and said unto them, 'What did Moses command you?' ⁴And they said, 'Moses suffered to write a bill of divorcement, and to put her away.' ⁵And Jesus answered and said unto them, 'For the hardness of your heart he wrote you this precept. ⁶ But from the beginning of the creation God made them male and female. ⁷ For this cause shall a man leave his father and mother, and cleave to his wife; ⁸and they twain shall be one flesh; so then they are no more twain, but one flesh. ⁹ What therefore God hath joined together, let not man put asunder.' ¹⁰And in the house his disciples asked him again of the same matter. ¹¹And he saith unto them, 'Whosoever shall put away his wife, and marry another, committeth adultery against her. ¹²And if a woman shall put away her husband, and be married to another, she committeth adultery.'

¹³And they brought young children to him, that he should touch them; and his disciples rebuked those that brought them. ¹⁴But when Jesus saw it, he was much displeased, and said unto them, 'Suffer the little children to come unto me, and forbid them not; for of such is the kingdom of God. ¹⁵Verily I say unto you, whosoever shall not receive the kingdom of God as a little child, he shall not enter therein.' ¹⁶And he took them up in his arms, put his hands upon them, and blessed them.

¹⁷And when he was gone forth into the way, there came one running, and kneeled to him, and asked him, 'Good Master, what shall I do that I may inherit eternal life?' ¹⁸And Jesus said unto him, 'Why callest thou me good? There is none good but one, that is, God. ¹⁹Thou knowest the commandments, "Do not commit adultery, Do not kill, Do not steal, Do not bear false witness, Defraud not, Honour thy father and mother."' ²⁰And he answered and said unto him, 'Master, all these have I observed from my youth.' ²¹Then Jesus beholding him loved him, and said unto him, 'One thing thou lackest: go thy way, sell whatsoever thou hast, and give to the poor, and thou shalt have treasure in heaven; and come, take up the cross, and follow me.' ²²And he was sad at that saying, and went away grieved; for he had great possessions.

²³And Jesus looked round about, and saith unto his disciples, 'How hardly shall they that have riches enter into the kingdom of God!' ²⁴And the disciples were astonished at his words. But Jesus answereth again, and saith unto them, 'Children, how hard is it for them that trust in riches to enter into the kingdom of God! ²⁵It is easier for a camel to go

through the eye of a needle, than for a rich man to enter into the kingdom of God.' ²⁶And they were astonished out of measure, saying among themselves, 'Who then can be saved?' ²⁷And Jesus looking upon them saith, 'With men it is impossible, but not with God; for with God all things are possible.'

²⁸ Then Peter began to say unto him, 'Lo, we have left all, and have followed thee.' ²⁹And Jesus answered and said, 'Verily I say unto you, there is no man that hath left house, or brethren, or sisters, or father, or mother, or wife, or children, or lands, for my sake, and the gospel's, ³⁰ but he shall receive an hundredfold now in this time, houses, and brethren, and sisters, and mothers, and children, and lands, with persecutions; and in the world to come eternal life. ³¹But many that are first shall be last; and the last first.'

³²And they were in the way going up to Jerusalem; and Jesus went before them; and they were amazed; and as they followed, they were afraid. And he took again the twelve, and began to tell them what things should happen unto him, ³³ saying, 'Behold, we go up to Jerusalem; and the Son of man shall be delivered unto the chief priests, and unto the scribes; and they shall condemn him to death, and shall deliver him to the Gentiles; ³⁴and they shall mock him, and shall scourge him, and shall spit upon him, and shall kill him: and the third day he shall rise again.'

³⁵And James and John, the sons of Zebedee, come unto him, saying, 'Master, we would that thou shouldest do for us whatsoever we shall desire.' ³⁶And he said unto them, 'What would ye that I should do for you?' ³⁷They said unto him, 'Grant unto us that we may sit, one on thy right hand,

and the other on thy left hand, in thy glory.' ³⁸ But Jesus said unto them, 'Ye know not what ye ask: can ye drink of the cup that I drink of? And be baptized with the baptism that I am baptized with?' ³⁹ And they said unto him, 'We can.' And Jesus said unto them, 'Ye shall indeed drink of the cup that I drink of; and with the baptism that I am baptized withal shall ye be baptized; ⁴⁰ but to sit on my right hand and on my left hand is not mine to give; but it shall be given to them for whom it is prepared.' ⁴¹ And when the ten heard it, they began to be much displeased with James and John. ⁴² But Jesus called them to him, and saith unto them, 'Ye know that they which are accounted to rule over the Gentiles exercise lordship over them; and their great ones exercise authority upon them. ⁴³ But so shall it not be among you; but whosoever will be great among you, shall be your minister; ⁴⁴ and whosoever of you will be the chiefest, shall be servant of all. ⁴⁵ For even the Son of man came not to be ministered unto, but to minister, and to give his life a ransom for many.'

⁴⁶ And they came to Jericho; and as he went out of Jericho with his disciples and a great number of people, blind Bartimæus, the son of Timæus, sat by the highway side begging. ⁴⁷ And when he heard that it was Jesus of Nazareth, he began to cry out, and say, 'Jesus, thou Son of David, have mercy on me.' ⁴⁸ And many charged him that he should hold his peace; but he cried the more a great deal, 'Thou Son of David, have mercy on me.' ⁴⁹ And Jesus stood still, and commanded him to be called. And they call the blind man, saying unto him, 'Be of good comfort, rise; he calleth thee.' ⁵⁰ And he, casting away his garment, rose, and came to Jesus. ⁵¹ And Jesus

answered and said unto him, 'What wilt thou that I should do unto thee?' The blind man said unto him, 'Lord, that I might receive my sight.' ⁵²And Jesus said unto him, 'Go thy way; thy faith hath made thee whole.' And immediately he received his sight, and followed Jesus in the way.

11 And when they came nigh to Jerusalem, unto Bethphage and Bethany, at the mount of Olives, he sendeth forth two of his disciples, ²and saith unto them, 'Go your way into the village over against you; and as soon as ye be entered into it, ye shall find a colt tied, whereon never man sat; loose him, and bring him. ³And if any man say unto you, "Why do ye this?" say ye that the Lord hath need of him; and straightway he will send him hither.' ⁴And they went their way, and found the colt tied by the door without in a place where two ways met; and they loose him. ⁵And certain of them that stood there said unto them, 'What do ye, loosing the colt?' ⁶And they said unto them even as Jesus had commanded; and they let them go. ⁷And they brought the colt to Jesus, and cast their garments on him; and he sat upon him. ⁸And many spread their garments in the way; and others cut down branches off the trees, and strawed them in the way. ⁹And they that went before, and they that followed, cried, saying, 'Hosanna; blessed is he that cometh in the name of the Lord; ¹⁰blessed be the kingdom of our father David, that cometh in the name of the Lord; hosanna in the highest.' ¹¹And Jesus entered into Jerusalem, and into the temple; and when he had looked round about upon all things, and now the eventide was come, he went out unto Bethany with the twelve.

¹²And on the morrow, when they were come from Bethany, he was hungry; ¹³and seeing a fig tree afar off having leaves, he came, if haply he might find any thing thereon; and when he came to it, he found nothing but leaves; for the time of figs was not yet. ¹⁴And Jesus answered and said unto it, 'No man eat fruit of thee hereafter for ever.' And his disciples heard it.

¹⁵And they come to Jerusalem; and Jesus went into the temple, and began to cast out them that sold and bought in the temple, and overthrew the tables of the moneychangers, and the seats of them that sold doves; ¹⁶and would not suffer that any man should carry any vessel through the temple. ¹⁷And he taught, saying unto them, 'Is it not written, "My house shall be called of all nations the house of prayer"? But ye have made it a den of thieves.' ¹⁸And the scribes and chief priests heard it, and sought how they might destroy him; for they feared him, because all the people was astonished at his doctrine. ¹⁹And when even was come, he went out of the city.

²⁰And in the morning, as they passed by, they saw the fig tree dried up from the roots. ²¹And Peter calling to remembrance saith unto him, 'Master, behold, the fig tree which thou cursedst is withered away.' ²²And Jesus answering saith unto them, 'Have faith in God. ²³For verily I say unto you, that whosoever shall say unto this mountain, "Be thou removed, and be thou cast into the sea"; and shall not doubt in his heart, but shall believe that those things which he saith shall come to pass; he shall have whatsoever he saith. ²⁴Therefore I say unto you, what things soever ye desire, when ye pray, believe that ye receive them, and ye shall have them. ²⁵And

when ye stand praying, forgive, if ye have ought against any: that your Father also which is in heaven may forgive you your trespasses. ²⁶But if ye do not forgive, neither will your Father which is in heaven forgive your trespasses.'

²⁷And they come again to Jerusalem; and as he was walking in the temple, there come to him the chief priests, and the scribes, and the elders, ²⁸and say unto him, 'By what authority doest thou these things? And who gave thee this authority to do these things?' ²⁹And Jesus answered and said unto them, 'I will also ask of you one question, and answer me, and I will tell you by what authority I do these things. ³⁰The baptism of John, was it from heaven, or of men? Answer me.' ³¹And they reasoned with themselves, saying, 'If we shall say, "From heaven," he will say, "Why then did ye not believe him?" ³²But if we shall say, "Of men,"' they feared the people; for all men counted John, that he was a prophet indeed.' ³³And they answered and said unto Jesus, 'We cannot tell.' And Jesus answering saith unto them, 'Neither do I tell you by what authority I do these things.'

12 And he began to speak unto them by parables. 'A certain man planted a vineyard, and set an hedge about it, and digged a place for the winefat, and built a tower, and let it out to husbandmen, and went into a far country. ²And at the season he sent to the husbandmen a servant, that he might receive from the husbandmen of the fruit of the vineyard. ³And they caught him, and beat him, and sent him away empty. ⁴And again he sent unto them another servant; and at him they cast stones, and wounded him in the head,

and sent him away shamefully handled. [5] And again he sent another; and him they killed, and many others; beating some, and killing some. [6] Having yet therefore one son, his wellbeloved, he sent him also last unto them, saying, "They will reverence my son." [7] But those husbandmen said among themselves, "This is the heir; come, let us kill him, and the inheritance shall be ours." [8] And they took him, and killed him, and cast him out of the vineyard. [9] What shall therefore the lord of the vineyard do? He will come and destroy the husbandmen, and will give the vineyard unto others. [10] And have ye not read this scripture: "The stone which the builders rejected is become the head of the corner. [11] This was the Lord's doing, and it is marvellous in our eyes"?' [12] And they sought to lay hold on him, but feared the people; for they knew that he had spoken the parable against them: and they left him, and went their way.

[13] And they send unto him certain of the Pharisees and of the Herodians, to catch him in his words. [14] And when they were come, they say unto him, 'Master, we know that thou art true, and carest for no man; for thou regardest not the person of men, but teachest the way of God in truth. Is it lawful to give tribute to Caesar, or not? [15] Shall we give, or shall we not give?' But he, knowing their hypocrisy, said unto them, 'Why tempt ye me? Bring me a penny, that I may see it.' [16] And they brought it. And he saith unto them, 'Whose is this image and superscription?' And they said unto him, 'Caesar's.' [17] And Jesus answering said unto them, 'Render to Caesar the things that are Caesar's, and to God the things that are God's.' And they marvelled at him.

¹⁸ Then come unto him the Sadducees, which say there is no resurrection; and they asked him, saying, ¹⁹ 'Master, Moses wrote unto us, "If a man's brother die, and leave his wife behind him, and leave no children, that his brother should take his wife, and raise up seed unto his brother." ²⁰ Now there were seven brethren; and the first took a wife, and dying left no seed. ²¹ And the second took her, and died, neither left he any seed; and the third likewise. ²² And the seven had her, and left no seed; last of all the woman died also. ²³ In the resurrection therefore, when they shall rise, whose wife shall she be of them? For the seven had her to wife.' ²⁴ And Jesus answering said unto them, 'Do ye not therefore err, because ye know not the scriptures, neither the power of God? ²⁵ For when they shall rise from the dead, they neither marry, nor are given in marriage; but are as the angels which are in heaven. ²⁶ And as touching the dead, that they rise; have ye not read in the book of Moses, how in the bush God spake unto him, saying, "I am the God of Abraham, and the God of Isaac, and the God of Jacob?" ²⁷ He is not the God of the dead, but the God of the living; ye therefore do greatly err.'

²⁸ And one of the scribes came, and having heard them reasoning together, and perceiving that he had answered them well, asked him, 'Which is the first commandment of all?' ²⁹ And Jesus answered him, 'The first of all the commandments is, "Hear, O Israel; the Lord our God is one Lord: ³⁰ and thou shalt love the Lord thy God with all thy heart, and with all thy soul, and with all thy mind, and with all thy strength": this is the first commandment. ³¹ And the second is like, namely this, "Thou shalt love thy neighbour as thyself." There

is none other commandment greater than these.' ³²And the scribe said unto him, 'Well, Master, thou hast said the truth: for there is one God; and there is none other but he; ³³and to love him with all the heart, and with all the understanding, and with all the soul, and with all the strength, and to love his neighbour as himself, is more than all whole burnt offerings and sacrifices.' ³⁴And when Jesus saw that he answered discreetly, he said unto him, 'Thou art not far from the kingdom of God.' And no man after that durst ask him any question.

³⁵And Jesus answered and said, while he taught in the temple, 'How say the scribes that Christ is the Son of David? ³⁶For David himself said by the Holy Ghost, "The Lord said to my Lord, 'Sit thou on my right hand, till I make thine enemies thy footstool.'" ³⁷David therefore himself calleth him "Lord"; and whence is he then his son?' And the common people heard him gladly.

³⁸And he said unto them in his doctrine, 'Beware of the scribes, which love to go in long clothing, and love salutations in the marketplaces, ³⁹and the chief seats in the synagogues, and the uppermost rooms at feasts, ⁴⁰which devour widows' houses, and for a pretence make long prayers: these shall receive greater damnation.'

⁴¹And Jesus sat over against the treasury, and beheld how the people cast money into the treasury; and many that were rich cast in much. ⁴²And there came a certain poor widow, and she threw in two mites, which make a farthing. ⁴³And he called unto him his disciples, and saith unto them, 'Verily I say unto you, that this poor widow hath cast more in, than all they which have cast into the treasury: ⁴⁴for all they did

cast in of their abundance; but she of her want did cast in all
that she had, even all her living.'

13 And as he went out of the temple, one of his disciples
saith unto him, 'Master, see what manner of stones and
what buildings are here!' ²And Jesus answering said unto
him, 'Seest thou these great buildings? There shall not be left
one stone upon another, that shall not be thrown down.'
³And as he sat upon the mount of Olives over against the
temple, Peter and James and John and Andrew asked him
privately, ⁴'Tell us, when shall these things be? And what
shall be the sign when all these things shall be fulfilled?'
⁵And Jesus answering them began to say, 'Take heed lest any
man deceive you; ⁶for many shall come in my name, saying,
"I am Christ," and shall deceive many. ⁷And when ye shall
hear of wars and rumours of wars, be ye not troubled; for
such things must needs be; but the end shall not be yet. ⁸For
nation shall rise against nation, and kingdom against kingdom; and there shall be earthquakes in divers places, and
there shall be famines and troubles: these are the beginnings
of sorrows.

⁹'But take heed to yourselves: for they shall deliver you
up to councils; and in the synagogues ye shall be beaten;
and ye shall be brought before rulers and kings for my sake,
for a testimony against them. ¹⁰And the gospel must first be
published among all nations. ¹¹But when they shall lead you,
and deliver you up, take no thought beforehand what ye
shall speak, neither do ye premeditate; but whatsoever shall
be given you in that hour, that speak ye: for it is not ye that

speak, but the Holy Ghost. ¹²Now the brother shall betray the brother to death, and the father the son; and children shall rise up against their parents, and shall cause them to be put to death. ¹³And ye shall be hated of all men for my name's sake: but he that shall endure unto the end, the same shall be saved.

¹⁴'But when ye shall see the abomination of desolation, spoken of by Daniel the prophet, standing where it ought not (let him that readeth understand) then let them that be in Judæa flee to the mountains; ¹⁵and let him that is on the house-top not go down into the house, neither enter therein, to take any thing out of his house; ¹⁶and let him that is in the field not turn back again for to take up his garment. ¹⁷But woe to them that are with child, and to them that give suck in those days! ¹⁸And pray ye that your flight be not in the winter. ¹⁹For in those days shall be affliction, such as was not from the beginning of the creation which God created unto this time, neither shall be. ²⁰And except that the Lord had shortened those days, no flesh should be saved; but for the elect's sake, whom he hath chosen, he hath shortened the days. ²¹And then if any man shall say to you, "Lo, here is Christ," or, "lo, he is there," believe him not; ²²for false Christs and false prophets shall rise, and shall shew signs and wonders, to seduce, if it were possible, even the elect. ²³But take ye heed: behold, I have foretold you all things.

²⁴'But in those days, after that tribulation, the sun shall be darkened, and the moon shall not give her light, ²⁵and the stars of heaven shall fall, and the powers that are in heaven shall be shaken. ²⁶And then shall they see the Son of man coming in the clouds with great power and glory. ²⁷And then

shall he send his angels, and shall gather together his elect from the four winds, from the uttermost part of the earth to the uttermost part of heaven. ²⁸ Now learn a parable of the fig tree: when her branch is yet tender, and putteth forth leaves, ye know that summer is near; ²⁹ so ye in like manner, when ye shall see these things come to pass, know that it is nigh, even at the doors. ³⁰ Verily I say unto you, that this generation shall not pass, till all these things be done. ³¹ Heaven and earth shall pass away: but my words shall not pass away.

³² 'But of that day and that hour knoweth no man, no, not the angels which are in heaven, neither the Son, but the Father. ³³ Take ye heed, watch and pray: for ye know not when the time is. ³⁴ For the Son of man is as a man taking a far journey, who left his house, and gave authority to his servants, and to every man his work, and commanded the porter to watch. ³⁵ Watch ye therefore: for ye know not when the master of the house cometh, at even, or at midnight, or at the cockcrowing, or in the morning, ³⁶ lest coming suddenly he find you sleeping. ³⁷ And what I say unto you I say unto all, Watch.'

14 After two days was the feast of the passover, and of unleavened bread; and the chief priests and the scribes sought how they might take him by craft, and put him to death. ² But they said, 'Not on the feast day, lest there be an uproar of the people.'

³ And being in Bethany in the house of Simon the leper, as he sat at meat, there came a woman having an alabaster box of ointment of spikenard very precious; and she brake the box, and poured it on his head. ⁴ And there were some

that had indignation within themselves, and said, 'Why was this waste of the ointment made?' ⁵For it might have been sold for more than three hundred pence, and have been given to the poor.' And they murmured against her. ⁶And Jesus said, 'Let her alone; why trouble ye her? She hath wrought a good work on me. ⁷For ye have the poor with you always, and whensoever ye will ye may do them good; but me ye have not always. ⁸She hath done what she could: she is come aforehand to anoint my body to the burying. ⁹Verily I say unto you, wheresoever this gospel shall be preached throughout the whole world, this also that she hath done shall be spoken of for a memorial of her.'

¹⁰And Judas Iscariot, one of the twelve, went unto the chief priests, to betray him unto them. ¹¹And when they heard it, they were glad, and promised to give him money. And he sought how he might conveniently betray him.

¹²And the first day of unleavened bread, when they killed the passover, his disciples said unto him, 'Where wilt thou that we go and prepare that thou mayest eat the passover?' ¹³And he sendeth forth two of his disciples, and saith unto them, 'Go ye into the city, and there shall meet you a man bearing a pitcher of water; follow him. ¹⁴And wheresoever he shall go in, say ye to the goodman of the house, "The Master saith, 'Where is the guestchamber, where I shall eat the passover with my disciples?'" ¹⁵And he will shew you a large upper room furnished and prepared; there make ready for us.' ¹⁶And his disciples went forth, and came into the city, and found as he had said unto them; and they made ready the passover. ¹⁷And in the evening he cometh with the twelve.

[18]And as they sat and did eat, Jesus said, 'Verily I say unto you, one of you which eateth with me shall betray me.' [19]And they began to be sorrowful, and to say unto him one by one, 'Is it I?' and another said, 'Is it I?' [20]And he answered and said unto them, 'It is one of the twelve, that dippeth with me in the dish. [21]The Son of man indeed goeth, as it is written of him; but woe to that man by whom the Son of man is betrayed! Good were it for that man if he had never been born.'

[22]And as they did eat, Jesus took bread, and blessed, and brake it, and gave to them, and said, 'Take, eat: this is my body.' [23]And he took the cup, and when he had given thanks, he gave it to them; and they all drank of it. [24]And he said unto them, 'This is my blood of the new testament, which is shed for many. [25]Verily I say unto you, I will drink no more of the fruit of the vine, until that day that I drink it new in the kingdom of God.'

[26]And when they had sung an hymn, they went out into the mount of Olives. [27]And Jesus saith unto them, 'All ye shall be offended because of me this night; for it is written, I will smite the shepherd, and the sheep shall be scattered. [28]But after that I am risen, I will go before you into Galilee.' [29]But Peter said unto him, 'Although all shall be offended, yet will not I.' [30]And Jesus saith unto him, 'Verily I say unto thee, that this day, even in this night, before the cock crow twice, thou shalt deny me thrice.' [31]But he spake the more vehemently, 'If I should die with thee, I will not deny thee in any wise.' Likewise also said they all. [32]And they came to a place which was named Gethsemane; and he saith to his disciples, 'Sit ye here, while I shall pray.' [33]And he taketh with

him Peter and James and John, and began to be sore amazed, and to be very heavy; ³⁴and saith unto them, 'My soul is exceeding sorrowful unto death; tarry ye here, and watch.' ³⁵And he went forward a little, and fell on the ground, and prayed that, if it were possible, the hour might pass from him. ³⁶And he said, 'Abba, Father, all things are possible unto thee; take away this cup from me; nevertheless not what I will, but what thou wilt.' ³⁷And he cometh, and findeth them sleeping, and saith unto Peter, 'Simon, sleepest thou? Couldest not thou watch one hour? ³⁸Watch ye and pray, lest ye enter into temptation. The spirit truly is ready, but the flesh is weak.' ³⁹And again he went away, and prayed, and spake the same words. ⁴⁰And when he returned, he found them asleep again (for their eyes were heavy), neither wist they what to answer him. ⁴¹And he cometh the third time, and saith unto them, 'Sleep on now, and take your rest: it is enough, the hour is come; behold, the Son of man is betrayed into the hands of sinners. ⁴²Rise up, let us go; lo, he that betrayeth me is at hand.'

⁴³And immediately, while he yet spake, cometh Judas, one of the twelve, and with him a great multitude with swords and staves, from the chief priests and the scribes and the elders. ⁴⁴And he that betrayed him had given them a token, saying, 'Whomsoever I shall kiss, that same is he; take him, and lead him away safely.' ⁴⁵And as soon as he was come, he goeth straightway to him, and saith, 'Master, master,' and kissed him.

⁴⁶And they laid their hands on him, and took him. ⁴⁷And one of them that stood by drew a sword, and smote a servant

of the high priest, and cut off his ear. ⁴⁸And Jesus answered and said unto them, 'Are ye come out, as against a thief, with swords and with staves to take me? ⁴⁹I was daily with you in the temple teaching, and ye took me not: but the scriptures must be fulfilled.' ⁵⁰And they all forsook him, and fled. ⁵¹And there followed him a certain young man, having a linen cloth cast about his naked body; and the young men laid hold on him; ⁵²and he left the linen cloth, and fled from them naked.

⁵³And they led Jesus away to the high priest; and with him were assembled all the chief priests and the elders and the scribes. ⁵⁴And Peter followed him afar off, even into the palace of the high priest: and he sat with the servants, and warmed himself at the fire. ⁵⁵And the chief priests and all the council sought for witness against Jesus to put him to death; and found none. ⁵⁶For many bare false witness against him, but their witness agreed not together. ⁵⁷And there arose certain, and bare false witness against him, saying, ⁵⁸'We heard him say, "I will destroy this temple that is made with hands, and within three days I will build another made without hands."' ⁵⁹But neither so did their witness agree together. ⁶⁰And the high priest stood up in the midst, and asked Jesus, saying, 'Answerest thou nothing? What is it which these witness against thee?' ⁶¹But he held his peace, and answered nothing. Again the high priest asked him, and said unto him, 'Art thou the Christ, the Son of the Blessed?' ⁶²And Jesus said, 'I am; and ye shall see the Son of man sitting on the right hand of power, and coming in the clouds of heaven.' ⁶³Then the high priest rent his clothes, and saith, 'What need we any further witnesses? ⁶⁴Ye have heard the blasphemy: what think

ye?' And they all condemned him to be guilty of death. ⁶⁵And some began to spit on him, and to cover his face, and to buffet him, and to say unto him, 'Prophesy,' and the servants did strike him with the palms of their hands.

⁶⁶And as Peter was beneath in the palace, there cometh one of the maids of the high priest; ⁶⁷and when she saw Peter warming himself, she looked upon him, and said, 'And thou also wast with Jesus of Nazareth.' ⁶⁸But he denied, saying, 'I know not, neither understand I what thou sayest.' And he went out into the porch; and the cock crew. ⁶⁹And a maid saw him again, and began to say to them that stood by, 'This is one of them.' ⁷⁰And he denied it again. And a little after, they that stood by said again to Peter, 'Surely thou art one of them; for thou art a Galilæan, and thy speech agreeth thereto.' ⁷¹But he began to curse and to swear, saying, 'I know not this man of whom ye speak.' ⁷²And the second time the cock crew. And Peter called to mind the word that Jesus said unto him, 'Before the cock crow twice, thou shalt deny me thrice.' And when he thought thereon, he wept.

15 And straightway in the morning the chief priests held a consultation with the elders and scribes and the whole council, and bound Jesus, and carried him away, and delivered him to Pilate. ²And Pilate asked him, 'Art thou the King of the Jews?' And he answering said unto him, 'Thou sayest it.' ³And the chief priests accused him of many things: but he answered nothing. ⁴And Pilate asked him again, saying, 'Answerest thou nothing? Behold how many things they witness against thee.' ⁵But Jesus yet answered nothing; so that

Pilate marvelled. ⁶Now at that feast he released unto them one prisoner, whomsoever they desired. ⁷And there was one named Barabbas, which lay bound with them that had made insurrection with him, who had committed murder in the insurrection. ⁸And the multitude crying aloud began to desire him to do as he had ever done unto them. ⁹But Pilate answered them, saying, 'Will ye that I release unto you the King of the Jews?' ¹⁰For he knew that the chief priests had delivered him for envy. ¹¹But the chief priests moved the people, that he should rather release Barabbas unto them. ¹²And Pilate answered and said again unto them, 'What will ye then that I shall do unto him whom ye call the King of the Jews?' ¹³And they cried out again, 'Crucify him.' ¹⁴Then Pilate said unto them, 'Why, what evil hath he done?' And they cried out the more exceedingly, 'Crucify him.'

¹⁵And so Pilate, willing to content the people, released Barabbas unto them, and delivered Jesus, when he had scourged him, to be crucified. ¹⁶And the soldiers led him away into the hall, called Prætorium; and they call together the whole band. ¹⁷And they clothed him with purple, and platted a crown of thorns, and put it about his head, ¹⁸and began to salute him, 'Hail, King of the Jews!' ¹⁹And they smote him on the head with a reed, and did spit upon him, and bowing their knees worshipped him. ²⁰And when they had mocked him, they took off the purple from him, and put his own clothes on him, and led him out to crucify him. ²¹And they compel one Simon a Cyrenian, who passed by, coming out of the country, the father of Alexander and Rufus, to bear his cross. ²²And they bring him unto the place Golgotha,

which is, being interpreted, 'The place of a skull.' ²³And they gave him to drink wine mingled with myrrh: but he received it not. ²⁴And when they had crucified him, they parted his garments, casting lots upon them, what every man should take. ²⁵And it was the third hour, and they crucified him. ²⁶And the superscription of his accusation was written over, 'The king of the Jews'. ²⁷And with him they crucify two thieves; the one on his right hand, and the other on his left. ²⁸And the scripture was fulfilled, which saith, 'And he was numbered with the transgressors.' ²⁹And they that passed by railed on him, wagging their heads, and saying, 'Ah, thou that destroyest the temple, and buildest it in three days, ³⁰save thyself, and come down from the cross.' ³¹Likewise also the chief priests mocking said among themselves with the scribes, 'He saved others; himself he cannot save. ³²Let Christ the King of Israel descend now from the cross, that we may see and believe.' And they that were crucified with him reviled him. ³³And when the sixth hour was come, there was darkness over the whole land until the ninth hour. ³⁴And at the ninth hour Jesus cried with a loud voice, saying, 'Eloi, Eloi, lama sabachthani?' which is, being interpreted, 'My God, my God, why hast thou forsaken me?' ³⁵And some of them that stood by, when they heard it, said, 'Behold, he calleth Elias.' ³⁶And one ran and filled a spunge full of vinegar, and put it on a reed, and gave him to drink, saying, 'Let alone; let us see whether Elias will come to take him down.' ³⁷And Jesus cried with a loud voice, and gave up the ghost. ³⁸And the veil of the temple was rent in twain from the top to the bottom.

³⁹And when the centurion, which stood over against him,

saw that he so cried out, and gave up the ghost, he said, 'Truly this man was the Son of God.' ⁴⁰ There were also women looking on afar off; among whom was Mary Magdalene, and Mary the mother of James the less and of Joses, and Salome ⁴¹(who also, when he was in Galilee, followed him, and ministered unto him), and many other women which came up with him unto Jerusalem.

⁴²And now when the even was come, because it was the preparation, that is, the day before the sabbath, ⁴³Joseph of Arimathæa, an honourable counsellor, which also waited for the kingdom of God, came, and went in boldly unto Pilate, and craved the body of Jesus. ⁴⁴And Pilate marvelled if he were already dead; and calling unto him the centurion, he asked him whether he had been any while dead. ⁴⁵And when he knew it of the centurion, he gave the body to Joseph. ⁴⁶And he bought fine linen, and took him down, and wrapped him in the linen, and laid him in a sepulchre which was hewn out of a rock, and rolled a stone unto the door of the sepulchre. ⁴⁷And Mary Magdalene and Mary the mother of Joses beheld where he was laid.

16 And when the sabbath was past, Mary Magdalene, and Mary the mother of James, and Salome, had bought sweet spices, that they might come and anoint him. ²And very early in the morning the first day of the week, they came unto the sepulchre at the rising of the sun. ³And they said among themselves, 'Who shall roll us away the stone from the door of the sepulchre?' ⁴And when they looked, they saw that the stone was rolled away; for it was very great.

⁵And entering into the sepulchre, they saw a young man sitting on the right side, clothed in a long white garment; and they were affrighted. ⁶And he saith unto them, 'Be not affrighted: ye seek Jesus of Nazareth, which was crucified. He is risen; he is not here; behold the place where they laid him. ⁷But go your way, tell his disciples and Peter that he goeth before you into Galilee: there shall ye see him, as he said unto you.' ⁸And they went out quickly, and fled from the sepulchre; for they trembled and were amazed; neither said they any thing to any man; for they were afraid.

 * ⁹Now when Jesus was risen early the first day of the week, he appeared first to Mary Magdalene, out of whom he had cast seven devils. ¹⁰And she went and told them that had been with him, as they mourned and wept. ¹¹And they, when they had heard that he was alive, and had been seen of her, believed not.

¹²After that he appeared in another form unto two of them, as they walked, and went into the country. ¹³And they went and told it unto the residue; neither believed they them.

¹⁴Afterward he appeared unto the eleven as they sat at meat, and upbraided them with their unbelief and hardness of heart, because they believed not them which had seen him after he was risen. ¹⁵And he said unto them, 'Go ye into all the world, and preach the gospel to every creature. ¹⁶He that believeth and is baptised shall be saved; but he that believeth not shall be damned. ¹⁷And these signs shall follow them that believe: in my name shall they cast out devils; they shall speak with new tongues; ¹⁸they shall take up serpents; and if they drink any deadly thing, it shall not hurt

them; they shall lay hands on the sick, and they shall recover.'

¹⁹ So then after the Lord had spoken unto them, he was received up into heaven, and sat on the right hand of God. ²⁰And they went forth, and preached every where, the Lord working with them, and confirming the word with signs following. Amen.

* *In the most reliable manuscripts Mark's gospel ends at ch. 16:8.*